Dearest
NEW YORK

A Love Letter to the Big Apple

Dearest
NEW YORK

A Love Letter to the Big Apple

DEIRDRE GARTNER

Globe Pequot

ESSEX, CONNECTICUT

Globe
Pequot

An imprint of Globe Pequot, the trade division of
The Rowman & Littlefield Publishing Group, Inc.
4501 Forbes Blvd., Ste. 200
Lanham, MD 20706
www.rowman.com

Distributed by NATIONAL BOOK NETWORK

Photography by Deirdre Gartner
Illustrations by Tracey Berglund, Arielle Pearl, and Katie Woodward

British Library Cataloguing in Publication Information available

Library of Congress Cataloging-in-Publication Data
Names: Gartner, Deirdre, author.
Title: Dearest New York : a love letter to the Big Apple / Deirdre Gartner.
Description: Essex, Connecticut : Globe Pequot, [2023] | Summary: "A
   compendium of starkly rich and uniquely personal images compiled from
   the author's 'Girl in the Yellow Taxi NYC' Instagram and blog. Includes
   photos, illustrations, and guides to both the classic and off-the-beat
   architectural wonders, cafes, shops, and hidden gems of New York City"—
   Provided by publisher.
Identifiers: LCCN 2023001172 (print) | LCCN 2023001173 (ebook) | ISBN
   9781493069262 (hardback) | ISBN 9781493069279 (epub)
Subjects: LCSH: New York (N.Y.)—Guidebooks. | New York (N.Y.)—Pictorial
   works.
Classification: LCC F128.18 .G29 2023 (print) | LCC F128.18 (ebook) | DDC
   974.7—dc23/eng/20230126
LC record available at https://lccn.loc.gov/2023001172
LC ebook record available at https://lccn.loc.gov/2023001173

Printed in India

Contents

Gems of New York

A Love Letter to the Big Apple

Dearest New York,

I want you to know how much you are loved by the world, but most especially, by me! You are a treasure trove of hidden gems, secluded alleyways, and bespoke shops. You are a city of dreams and dreamers replete with endless possibilities. Every inch of you has been photographed and filmed throughout the years, and yet I never tire of seeing new images of you. You are a study in constant motion, always evolving. No matter where else I may travel, there is still nothing more beautiful than your glistening skyline at sunset.

I love that you are a glorious one-of-a-kind melting pot with over 800 languages spoken throughout your mystical, magical landscape.

I love that you are a city without judgment opening your arms to the creative and the eccentric—a city where all things are possible for everyone.

I love that I get to taste the finest cuisines from Kathmandu to Timbuktu, sample wines of acclaimed sommeliers and rooftop

growers alike, be entertained by the world renowned or the enterprising kid on the corner. I can visit the finest perfumeries on the Upper East Side while sampling spices of ancient civilizations on the Lower East Side all in the same day!

You are a city of dichotomies: exhilarating and exhausting, humbling and arrogant, quietly inspiring while loudly provoking. You are in perpetual transition and a glorious example of extraordinary resilience.

My hope in presenting this little book is that I have captured your unique essence and beauty. You are my beloved city, with quirks aplenty like all the rest of us yet perfect in every way.

I will always be forever yours,

xoxo

to:
New York City
with
love

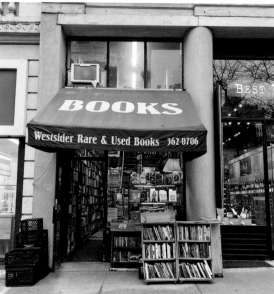

NEIGHBORHOODS

Upper East Side

The Upper East Side

Some of the most famous families have made their homes on New York's Upper East Side including the Roosevelts, Kennedys, Rockefellers, and Carnegies. These tycoons were among an elite group of real estate pioneers in the early 1900s who developed this storied neighborhood into what it is today. Quiet tree-lined streets, cute cafes, Michelin star–rated restaurants, designer shopping, Central Park, and some of the best museums in the world are what you will find on the Upper East Side.

Spanning from 59th Street to 96th Street between the East River and Central Park, the Upper East Side is a combination of three sub-neighborhoods. There's the more laid back Yorkville section to the east where stands Gracie Mansion, home to the mayor of New York City. The Lenox Hill area borders Central Park with ultra-glamorous residences, while Carnegie Hill, running from 86th through 98th Streets just off Park Avenue, features Neo-Gothic mansions and brownstones.

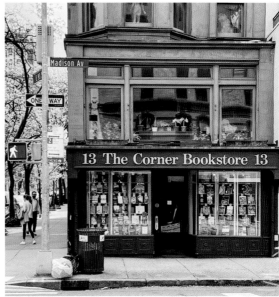

Calling all Coffee Lovers

Ralph's Coffee

"As long as there was coffee in the world, how bad could things be?"

— Cassandra Clare, City of Ashes

Caffe Reggio

Caffe Dante

Maman

787 Coffee

Be Strong, I Whispered to My Coffee

Whether you enjoy a cold brew, latte, double espresso,
cappuccino, or just a simple cup of coffee, in New York City,
there's no shortage of cozy neighborhood coffee shops.

Favorite NYC Spots for a Heavenly Cup of Joe

CAFFE DANTE, 79 MacDougal St.

CAFFE REGGIO, 119 MacDougal St.

INTELLIGENTSIA COFFEE @ THE HIGHLINE HOTEL, 180 10th Ave.

LAUGHING MAN CAFÉ, 184 Duane St.

MAMAN, my favorite location is 239 Centre St.

MUD, 307 East 9th St.

BAR PISSELLINO, 52 Grove St.

RALPH'S COFFEE, my favorite location is 888 Madison Ave.

ROSECRANS, 7 Greenwich Ave.

787 COFFEE, my favorite location is 228 East 80th St.

The perfect day (or two) on the Upper East Side starts with an early morning walk in Central Park. Arriving in the park along with the dog walkers and runners, there's just nothing more beautiful and breathtaking than seeing the park come to life with all the sights and sounds.

Exit the park at 72nd Street and head to Madison Avenue where Ralph's Coffee has the perfect combination of good coffee, croissants, and people watching.

Albertine Books is worth a pop-in. Located in the historic Payne Whitney Mansion on Fifth Avenue and 79th Street, this literary gem is the only book shop in New York devoted solely to books printed in French and English. Head up to the second floor and curl up in one of their old leather chairs tucked under a ceiling of celestial stars.

Wander down the streets from the 90s to the 60s and between Fifth and Madison Avenues where you will see some of the most beautiful and historic homes and townhouses in the city. Museum Mile, which starts at 82nd Street and Fifth Avenue and goes all the way up to 110th Street, is home to world class museums, such as the Museum of the City of New York, the Frick, the Guggenheim, the Metropolitan Museum of Art, and my favorite, the Cooper Hewitt (America's only museum dedicated solely to design, in Andrew Carnegie's former mansion).

There are many wonderful restaurants and cafes around where you can grab lunch, but I prefer to go old school. Lexington Candy Shop, at 83rd Street and Lexington Avenue (just 3 blocks from the Met) is a neighborhood staple that has been serving up tuna melts, cheeseburgers, and egg-creams since 1925. Sit at the soda counter for the authentic "stepping back in time" experience.

Walk off your lunch with a stroll to Carl Schurz Park. Tucked along the East River at 86th Street, this lesser-known gem of a park has two dog runs, panoramic river views, and flower gardens that overflow in the summer with hibiscus, canna lilies, and dahlias the size of dinner plates.

One of my favorite things to do on a clear day is to take a ride on the Roosevelt Island Tram, praised by the *New York Times* as "the most exciting view in New York City." In just 4 minutes and the cost of a single swipe on your MTA card, you can travel from busy Manhattan to quiet, beautiful, residential Roosevelt Island, home to Franklin Roosevelt Four Freedoms Park, remnants of a former smallpox hospital, and a beautiful lighthouse. When you arrive off the tram, there is a visitor center where you can pick up a map to help you explore the island. When you get off the tram back on the Manhattan side, head down the block to Serendipity 3 at 225 East 60th St. This restaurant has the sweetest treats in town. Beloved by celebrities, tourists, and this homegrown New Yorker, Serendipity 3 proves that the joy of a frozen dessert can be life changing. What's not to love about an oversized sundae, banana split, or their famous frozen hot chocolate?

Central Park

The Ever-Enchanting Central Park

Trying to describe the singular sensation that is Central Park is like trying to describe well, life itself! Each one of the park's 843 acres is a most coveted haven from the madness of Manhattan, containing a treasure trove of art, entertainment, culinary delights, people watching, and nature. It's what separates this city—both literally and figuratively—from any other public space in the world. No visit to the Big Apple would be complete without a long, leisurely stroll through this gem—truly New York's jewel in the crown.

Where to begin suggestions for visiting the park, that capture the spirit, sights, and sounds of this magical wonderland? Maybe head to Shakespeare Garden where you will find 4 acres of gorgeous plantings that change with the season, take a spin on the famous carousel, or a photo in front of one of the 70 sculptures that are scattered throughout the park? Aaaagh. There are far too many to enumerate, so just start wandering.

Maja And Bessie Sullivan
Two Incredible Ladies
Thank You For Your Kindness
Compassion Friendship And Love

How to spend the perfect day in
Central Park

Take an early morning walk around the reservoir

PICNIC ON THE GREAT LAWN

See the sea lions being fed at the zoo

RENT A ROWBOAT

Snap a photo of the Imagine Mosaic

Soak in the beauty of the conservatory gardens

WATCH THE SUNSET FROM BELVEDERE CASTLE

Book a table for dinner at Tavern On The Green

Conservatory Garden

One of the hidden wonders of Central Park is the Conservatory Garden at Fifth Avenue and 105th Street, a secluded 6-acre oasis, just a few steps down from one of the city's busiest thoroughfares. It is the only formal garden found in Central Park. The quiet, calm atmosphere of the garden free from runners and cyclists make it an ideal spot for weddings and relaxing afternoon walks. The garden is divided into three different sections each representing its own specific style: the north (French Garden), central (Italian Garden), and south (English Garden).

Wondering Where You Are in the Park?

If you ever lose your sense of direction in the park, head to the nearest lamp post or "luminaries" as they are called. There are 1,600 throughout the park and each can tell your whereabouts. On the post you will see four numbers. The first two digits tell you the nearest street and the second set will tell you whether you are on the East or West Side. Even numbers mean east, odd numbers west.

Central Park Zoo

snow leopards
penguins & sea birds
red pandas
snow monkeys
sea lions
central gardens
tropic zone
intelligence garden

The Central Park Zoo

What do a special group of tropical birds, snow leopards, grizzly bears, and even one of the nation's largest colonies of Antarctic penguins have in common? They all call New York's fabled Central Park Zoo their home.

Back in the 1870s New Yorkers began dropping off their unwanted pets at The Arsenal, an old Gothic-style former munitions building which predates the park.

The abandoned menagerie of animals included 72 white swans along with a newborn black bear cub. A zoo was thus born! Today it is operated by the Wildlife Conservation Society and is actively involved in the preservation of endangered species.

Be sure to stop by the zoo as you stroll through Central Park. You won't want to miss the sassy sea lions at feeding time or the snow leopard, who is a wonder to behold especially in the midst of our concrete jungle! And don't forget the Children's Zoo for the wee ones (or just for your own inner child).

Upper West Side

The Upper West Side

Framed within the iconic pastures of Central and Riverside Park, from 59th Street to 110th Street, the Upper West Side neighborhood exudes a more relaxed, slower-paced, low-key feel. Stroll down the tree-lined streets and admire the diverse architecture. Dating back to the 1800s, rows of historic brownstones are anchored with larger iconic structures like the Dakota, New York's first luxury apartment building built in 1884 and the San Remo, the first twin-towered building to rise in the city, built in 1930. It is also home to Lincoln Center, the cornerstone to New York City's culture and one of the most inspiring places to see dance, music, or theater performed. No trip to the Upper West Side would be complete without stopping into the Museum of Natural History to see the towering T-Rex or 94-foot-long blue whale that is suspended from the ceiling. These landmarks mixed in with mom-and-pop stores, lively bars, and sidewalk cafes make this neighborhood feel as much a mindset as it does a physical place.

There is no better way to start the day on the Upper West Side than with a stop at Zabar's, at 80th Street and Broadway. This gourmet deli and grocer has been in the same location for more than 80 years. Order their famous bagel with smoked fish, chocolate babka, a cup of coffee, and head to Riverside Park for a picturesque morning stroll and a dose of tranquility. Next, head to the Museum of Natural History located on Central Park West and 79th Street. Spanning 4 city blocks, this museum is a New York icon. On your way to the museum see if you can find one of the few remaining works by famed artist Banksy. *Hammer Boy* is a whimsical image of a boy hammering a fire standpipe at 79th Street east of Broadway. Plan to spend a couple of hours (at least) at the museum, then head across the street to New York's oldest museum, the New York Historical Society, home to an extensive collection of artifacts, sculptures, and one of the largest collections of Tiffany lamps.

If you happen to be in the Upper West Side neighborhood on a Sunday, check out Grand Bazaar NYC, at 77th Street and Columbus Avenue. It is a great place to find a one-of-a-kind mix of jewelry, vintage items, home goods, antiques, and artisanal foods. What began in the early 1980s as a yard sale for parents to raise money for their children's school is now the oldest shopping market in New York City. Bookworms should schedule a pit-stop at The Strand, at 81st Street and Columbus Avenue. This sibling to the iconic flagship store on East 12th Street has the same amazing combination of new, used, and rare books of all genres. You'll wonder where the time flew after perusing the shelves. As the sun sets change into your best evening wear and head to Lincoln Center (one of my favorite spots) for an evening of unrivaled entertainment. Purchase tickets for a performance at the New York City Ballet, New York Philharmonic, Metropolitan Opera, Lincoln Center Theater, or just spend the evening sitting by the fountain taking in the beauty of this New York gem!

Fun Facts About New York City's Most Famous Icons

- The pigeon is the city's most iconic species of wildlife and has truly become a quintessential New York character. The population in NYC is estimated to exceed more than one million.

- The seven spikes in the Statue of Liberty's crown represent the seven seas, seven continents, and the ray of the sun.

- Central Parks Bethesda Fountain was created by Emma Stebbins, the first woman artist to be commissioned by the city and have her art used in a public space.

- The Staten Island Ferry has been in use since 1905. A glorious 5-mile, 25-minute mini cruise with great views of the Statue of Liberty, Lower Manhattan, and the New York Harbor—the best part, it's FREE.

- There are a little more than 13,000 yellow taxis in NYC each making about 800 trips per month.

- If all the tracks that make up the New York City subway system were laid end to end, they would stretch from New York to Chicago.

- Hot dog carts are a ubiquitous sight in New York City. The National Hot Dog and Sausage Council estimates that New Yorkers spend over $120 million a year on franks.

Midtown

Midtown

If New York is the "Big Apple," then Midtown Manhattan is most definitely the core. Filled with noise, crowds, colorful characters, and home to some of the city's most iconic and popular tourist attractions, the Midtown area, by right of its location, also provides easy accessibility to other parts of the city.

Midtown is where you will find famous architectural landmarks like Grand Central Terminal, the Chrysler Building, the Museum of Modern Art, and Rockefeller Center. Also in the area is Radio City Music Hall, home to the famous Rockettes and a great place to see concerts. Tourists flock to Broadway, the epicenter of the city's theater district. Of course, no New Year's Eve would be complete without the annual ritual of large crowds gathering in the chaos of Times Square to ring in the New Year. Midtown Manhattan is the neighborhood most people first envision when they think of New York.

Times Square

"The soul of Times Square remains intact. The neon still sparkles. Tourists still wander around bewildered. The whiff of last night's junk food still hangs in the air."

—*Nicolai Ouroussoff*

Times Square can be described as vibrant, honky-tonk, messy, chaotic, and at the same time magical. Home to a variety of activities ranging from street performers, art installations, concerts, and theater to shopping and dining, it has something for everyone. It is often called the "crossroads of the world" and on any given day you can see why. It is one of the world's most visited tourist attractions drawing an estimated 50 million visitors annually. Brightly lit by billboards and advertisements, its iconic imagery makes it the first place many people identify New York City with, especially on New Year's Eve.

Times Square is also home to New York City's theater district commonly known as "Broadway." This is where everyone in showbiz goes to make their mark. There are 41 Broadway theaters, but many of the city's most innovative and engaging new plays and musicals can be found off-Broadway. Here in these more intimate spaces, you'll find presentations of work in a wide range of styles which usually cost less than a show on the "Great White Way." My view is that all theater is good theater, but a Broadway show should be on everyone's bucket list.

To Your Cart's Delight

Street cart vendors are part of New York City's cultural fabric, with about 20,000 throughout NYC. Eating from a street cart is a must-do New York experience and every New Yorker has their favorite cart.

The Breakfast Cart features an assortment of breakfast treats and depending on which cart you go to a strong cup of joe served in one of those blue and white Greek cups that read "WE ARE HAPPY TO SERVE YOU." Pastries are usually about the size of a dinner plate and topped with a sugary glaze (perfect power breakfast). You'll also find pre-buttered bagels and an assortment of breakfast sandwiches.

The Hot Dog Cart serves up the classic New York food experience, the dirty water dog. Named after the warm, salty water it's cooked in, the dog is served in a soft bun with topping of your choice: mustard, sauerkraut, ketchup, or a must-try NY original, the tomato and onion relish. You'll find the ubiquitous Sabrett hot dog carts with their blue and yellow awnings scattered throughout this city.

The Pretzel Cart, one of the unofficial symbols of the Big Apple, can be found on many street corners, mostly concentrated in Midtown. Generous in size and equally filling, this New York staple is a meal in and of itself. If you want your pretzel a little warmer, most vendors will happily warm them up for you the old-fashioned way right under the flame. Word of advice: Should you get a pretzel that seems a tad on the stale side (part of the experience), most vendors will exchange your pretzel.

The Halal Guys. If you are looking for a full-fledged meal, there are plenty of options from the food trucks and street carts who make some of the best ethnic food in town. One can savor authentic Greek, Mexican, Thai, and Ethiopian delights all in the space of a few blocks. For Middle Eastern food it's The Halal Guys who score the top prize. The original carts in Midtown (at 53rd Street and Sixth Avenue) have been around since 1990 serving up delicious, filling dishes. Make sure to try their signature chicken over rice platter with a secret white sauce. Warning: There is usually a long line in front of the cart, but it's worth the wait!

New York Public Library:
A Peaceful Oasis on Fifth Avenue

When you walk up the majestic steps at 42nd Street and Fifth Avenue, you enter the legendary main branch of the New York Public Library. Free to enter and explore, this often-overlooked museum is a refuge for New Yorkers who need a quiet place to read, think, or just be. Since its founding in 1895, millions of visitors have marveled over the wonders of the library's architectural magnificence and gleaned inspiration from its trove of resources. The marble lions proudly guarding the New York Public Library at Fifth Avenue are named "Patience" and "Fortitude." Often called New York's most lovable public sculptures, the lions have been photographed alongside countless tourists, replicated as bookends, illustrated in numerous children's books, and served as the backdrop for many high-profile films such as *The Wiz*, *King Kong*, *13 Going on 30*, and *Spider-Man*.

Make sure to visit the majestic Rose Reading Room. The extraordinary 52-foot-tall ceilings display murals of vibrant skies and billowing clouds. When you leave the library head down 41st Street between Park and Fifth Avenues. Make sure to check out the pavement where you will find 44 beautifully sculpted bronze plaques with inspirational quotes and whimsical illustrations—named "Library Way." This is our city's homage to the world's greatest literary highlights.

Bryant Park

Just behind the New York Public Library is Bryant Park—an oasis of peace and calm smack dab in the middle of Manhattan. It is the perfect spot to meet friends, eat lunch, chat, stroll, read a book, take a spin on the carousel, or simply sit and think. The park annually hosts over 1,000 free activities, classes, and events. From ice skating and curling in the winter to movie nights, concerts, and yoga classes in the summer, this park has something for New Yorkers and visitors to love throughout the season.

Fun Facts: New York Public Library

- Some of the most beloved films of the past 50 years have used its exquisite interiors as backdrops. *Breakfast at Tiffany's*, *The Thomas Crown Affair*, *Ghostbusters*, and Carrie Bradshaw's iconic yet ill-fated wedding from TV's *Sex and the City* were all shot here.

- The library has approximately 45,000 menus dating back all the way from the 1840s to the present, one of the largest collections in the world.

- Some of the treasures tucked away at the library are Charles Dickens's writing desk, a handwritten poem by Emily Dickinson, and George Washington's recipe for beer.

- The Map Room holds one of the most impressive collections in the world containing over 433,000 sheet maps and 20,000 books, and atlases spanning from the 15th century to the present.

THE HIGHLINE HOTEL

Chelsea

Chelsea

Located west of Broadway across to the Hudson River from 14th to West 30th Street, the neighborhood of Chelsea has seen its share of transformations over time. Beginning in the late 1800s this West Side neighborhood was primarily an industrial center. The Nabisco Company opened its first factory here. Just a few decades later, the first railroad in the United States established their tracks in this same district. Yet as years passed, this area saw its share of degradation and became just another dark, lifeless piece of NYC history for a time.

But this city is always reinventing itself—change is in her DNA. What was once a seemingly desolate neighborhood has in recent years become one of the most sought-after places to live in Manhattan. Chelsea has experienced an extraordinary renaissance, buzzing with art/cultural activity (including a floating park named "Little Island") and home to some of the city's most charming shops, restaurants, and bakeries.

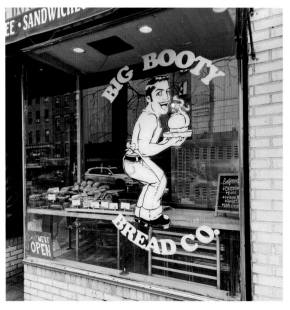

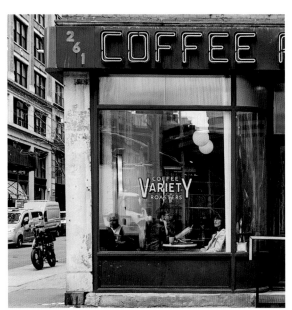

Stroll the Chelsea Historic District, running from West 20th Street to West 22nd Street, between Eighth and Ninth Avenues. These charming blocks of townhouses in varying styles of Italianate, Greek Revival, and other popular architectural styles of the 19th century practically ooze with New York history. It's almost impossible to keep your imagination in check envisioning what the city was like back in the day.

A favorite hangout of musicians, actors, and literary and fine artists such as Andy Warhol, Bob Dylan, Jimi Hendrix, and Janis Joplin, the Chelsea Hotel on 23rd Street is among the premier cultural sights in New York. The hotel was designated a New York City landmark in 1966.

The Joyce Theater, a 472-seat dance performance venue at 175 Eighth Avenue, is arguably a leading presenter of dance in New York City and internationally. While the Art Moderne 1941 building began as a movie theater featuring cult films and revivals, it has since become the venue to see world-renowned dance companies performing modern dance, ballet, flamenco, and tango at affordable prices.

While in Chelsea, make sure to take in a performance at the award-winning off-Broadway Atlantic Theater Company. Located in the parish hall of St. Peter's Episcopal Church on West 20th Street, this small intimate theater brings innovative, engaging plays to New York City for much less than the cost of a Broadway show.

Gallery Hopping in Chelsea

Whatever your personal, objective, or subjective take on art is, it's all here in Chelsea. Teeming with over 200 galleries (many of which are housed in creatively converted warehouses), Chelsea is one big museum representing a veritable potpourri of avant-garde, established, and up-and-coming artists. With many galleries to choose from, the best tactic is to window shop their storefronts, ambling up and down the blocks between 18th and 27th Streets between Tenth and Eleventh Avenues. You, quite literally, get a free pass to seeing some of the world's most spectacular art.

For good measure, end your gallery day in Chelsea with a few of my personal favorite museums. The Rubin Museum, renowned for its collection of Himalayan art, offers additional diverse, provocative exhibits and programs including film, live discussion, and concerts. The Museum at The Fashion Institute of Technology ("FIT") always features inspiring exhibits on the history and future of fashion.

Street Art by Kobra

As you wander around New York, you are sure to come across the work of one of the most recognizable and celebrated muralists of our time, Brazilian artist Eduardo Kobra. Kobra spent 5 months creating 18 large-scale murals throughout the city. His "Colors of Freedom" series features a call to action for peace and positive change in the world. Three of his pieces are in Chelsea. *We Love NY* is on the corner of 21st Street and Eighth Avenue. *Tolerance* is on 18th Street and Tenth Avenue, and *Mount Rushmore* is above the historic Empire Diner on 23rd Street and Tenth Avenue.

Influenced early in his life by artists like Keith Haring, Andy Warhol, and Jean-Michel Basquiat, Kobra chose New York for this colossal project as a nod to the city where street art originated.

The High Line

Once an elevated railway that sat abandoned on the West Side for decades, the High Line has become one of the city's most popular tourist attractions. Converted to a coveted public park, the High Line sits 30 feet above street level and stretches from Gansevort Street all the way up to 34th Street. While you can spend your entire time on the High Line taking in the beauty of the plantings and spectacular city views, breathe in all the public art that surrounds you. High Line Art (founded in 2009 by Friends of the High Line) invites artists to engage in the uniqueness of commissions, exhibitions, and performances.

The High Line Hotel

In a quiet pocket of Chelsea sits the Federal-style landmark that is the High Line Hotel. This gem of an edifice is where 19th-century writer Clement C. Moore wrote "A Visit from St. Nicholas," and trust me, you feel his inspiration within these walls. The visitor is transported to a bygone era with its Gothic-inspired brick buildings and original details including sumptuous fireplaces and detailed moldings. Today the hotel has been reimagined by the legendary design firm Roman & Williams. Oriental rugs, 1920s rotary phones, old typewriters, and beautiful Victorian antiques combine to create a sophisticated throwback vibe. Stop in for a latte from the Intelligentsia lobby bar and don't forget your furry friends, as all dogs are welcome. If these walls could talk!

Eat and Shop Your Way through Chelsea Market

What was once the National Biscuit Company factory complex (the very same company that created the iconic Oreo cookie) is now the Chelsea Market. Occupying an entire city block on Ninth Avenue between 15th and 16th Streets, the building still maintains many original architectural vestiges (original floors, exposed brick) from its storied past. Today it houses a food hall, shops, offices, and a television production facility. Make sure you arrive with an empty stomach as the dizzying array of culinary choices are endless. With tacos, lobster rolls, ramen, doughnuts, cheese, and churros, this is a foodie's heaven. Walk off some of those delectable delights with a bit of shopping therapy. Pearl River Market sells everything from one-of-a-kind items imported from Asia (jade jewelry, chopsticks, slippers, rice cakes, etc.) as well as innovative merchandise designed and created by Asian American designers. Artists & Fleas, on the southwest corner of the market, features an ongoing rotation of authentically original artists and vendors selling unique offerings in fashion, vintage clothing, records, art, design, and more. As one of the few places to purchase one-of-a-kind, inventive, and truly cool merchandise, Artists & Fleas is a paradise for buyers, trendsetters, and creative entrepreneurs alike.

New Yorkers on What They Love Most About NYC

"New York City is the capital of everything with a tapestry of rich, multicultural experiences across its five boroughs—it's a place uniquely defined by its boundless energy, infectious magnetism, and welcoming spirit."

—Chris Heywood, EVP, Global Communications,
NYC & Company

"New York City is for the humans who know how to turn the tidal wave of the city's energy in their favor . . . so that the rush of those around them propels them forward instead of holding them back."

—Lauren Lovette, former Principal Dancer NYCB,
Resident Choreographer, Paul Taylor Dance Company

"There is no place like it. There's even a strange beauty to the noise, chaos, and craziness. As a professional musician, I've toured through all 50 states and have never been in a city that I'd rather live in. I miss it when I'm away and feel at home as soon as I get back."

—Steve Holloway, Broadway musician

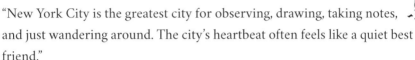

"New York City is the greatest city for observing, drawing, taking notes, and just wandering around. The city's heartbeat often feels like a quiet best friend."

—Tracey Berglund, Artist

"Growing up in an apartment I had the advantage of having the city as my backyard. From Central Park to Washington Square Park and everything in between was my playground. I love that New York is truly a unique melting pot that never ceases to amaze, impress, and inspire me"

—Thomas Whitburn, NYC Beekeeper, Best Bees Company

"I love that New York City is kind to the elderly. It has ramps on street corners, elevators in subway stations, and lots of benches to sit and observe the city in motion."

—Sam Gross, Cartoonist, *The New Yorker*

"The Village": Greenwich Village & West Village

Greenwich Village

The epicenter of the city's 1960s counterculture movement, Greenwich Village is now a hub of popular cafes, restaurants, jazz clubs, off-Broadway theaters, New York University buildings, and the beautiful Washington Square Park.

West Village

Encompassing about half the size of Greenwich Village and where most of the streets are no longer on a grid, the West Village is a study in old-world charm contrasted with a progressive future focus. With a quaint patchwork of 19th-century architecture, tree-lined, angled, and often cobblestoned streets and public squares, cozy cafes, and specialty shops, it's easy to feel as if you're on a movie set about a bygone era of New York City. Dig a bit deeper and you'll understand how this diverse patch of the city became the epicenter of a flourishing art scene as well as the springboard for the gay rights movement. The West Village is at once sophisticated and bohemian.

Wear your most comfortable shoes as this intimate gem of a neighborhood is made for strolling! Start your day with a leisurely walk across iconic Washington Square Park. Grab a cappuccino at Cafe Reggio—one of the area's oldest cafes. For lunchtime your options are endless—Boucherie, Buvette, and Little Owl among them. As for an authentically unique shopping experience, a few of my personal favorite haunts include the Three Lives & Company bookstore, John Derian for a preciously curated selection of home goods and decor, and Greenwich Letterpress, my go-to for whimsical cards, stationery, and gifts. As dusk approaches so does cocktail hour! Head over to Bar Pisellino for one of their infamous Negronis. From there, check out The Waverly Inn for dinner (call in advance to be on the safe side). Hear the clinking of glasses and chatter of gossip—a great place for family and friends to celebrate a special occasion or just a fun night of being together. And finally, no West Village experience would be complete without a savory slice of heaven from the legendary Joe's Pizza to satiate those late-night cravings.

Fun Facts

- There are over 800 languages spoken in NYC.

- NYC is the home to the first-ever US pizzeria, Lombardi's, opened in 1895.

- The Empire State Building gets hit by lightning around 23 times a year.

Grove Street

With all the myriad streets to stroll in the city, Grove Street has to be one of my favorites. Although very short in length (a span of only 5 blocks), it is very long in character. An abundance of Federal-style brownstones and the rare all-wooden home at 17 Grove capture the imagination of a long-ago yet still wonderfully vibrant West Village. Check out the now-iconic building portrayed in the hit television series *Friends*, on the corner of Grove and Bedford Street. Note the fire engine red facade on the ground floor—home to the Little Owl restaurant—perfect for brunch and people watching!

Grove Court

Nestled between 10 and 12 Grove Street is Grove Court—a private little Shangri-La shared by six beautiful red brick townhouses and set back from the main street. Built in 1854, its cobblestone path leads to a sweet garden filled with seasonal flowers and decorative touches during the holidays. Truly an enchanted garden.

Christopher Street

Not only is Christopher Street one of the oldest streets in the West Village, it is also one of the most colorful. With a plethora of unique shops and restaurants, it is the embodiment of old-world charm meets 21st-century innovation. Bursting with bold creativity, Christopher Street became the historical hub of gay rights in New York City when in the early hours of June 28, 1969, police officers raided the Stonewall Inn. It marked the first time that a unified gay community took action in letting the authorities know they were no longer willing to participate in their own persecution. That night launched Stonewall Inn's reputation as the birthplace of the gay rights movement, and it continues to be the cultural epicenter for the LGBTQ community.

Gay Street

Originally a horse stable alleyway, Gay Street—extending just 1 block from Christopher Street to Waverly Place—is a quaint, picturesque gem of a street. Featured in numerous films and music videos, it's also, not surprisingly, one of the most photographed streets in New York City.

Green Escapes

When living in, or touring the "concrete jungle" that is New York City, it is comforting to know that you can always head for greener pastures scattered among the asphalt metropolis. A few in the West Village include:

Jefferson Market Garden, 70 A Greenwich Ave.

Walk around the brick path that circles the lawn, smell the fragrant roses, count the fish in the koi pond, or simply sit on one of the benches and enjoy the beautiful surroundings.

The Gardens at St. Luke in the Fields, 485 Hudson St.

Comprising more than two-thirds of an acre, this oasis is filled with trees, wildflowers, blooming bushes, and manicured gardens that attract over 100 species of birds and 24 types of butterflies. "St. Luke"—a little piece of heaven on the West Village earth!

Abington Square Park, Hudson Street, Eighth Avenue, West 12th Street

One of the oldest and smallest parks, this bucolic little patch of greenery is just what you need to decompress with a hot cup of coffee and a good book.

Jefferson Market Garden

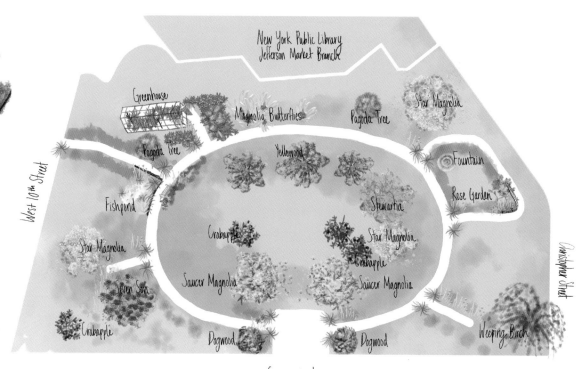

New York Public Library
Jefferson Market Branch

Greenhouse

Magnolia Butterflies

Pagoda Tree

Star Magnolia

Pagoda Tree

Yellowwood

Fountain

West 10th Street

Fishpond

Stewartia

Rose Garden

Crabapple

Star Magnolia

Star Magnolia

Seven Son

Crabapple

Saucer Magnolia

Saucer Magnolia

Christopher Street

Crabapple

Dogwood

Dogwood

Weeping Birch

Greenwich Avenue

Perry Street

With its dense foliage and exquisite brownstones, Perry Street is among the most iconic addresses in the heart of the West Village.

Years after the hit television series ended, 64 Perry St. will always be associated with *Sex and the City*, among its ardent fans. After all, the facade of this townhouse was used to depict the home of the show's heroine and NYC-obsessed column writer, Carrie Bradshaw.

Head further down to 88 Perry St. and take note of the stunning blue and white tile archway—a beloved landmark since the 1970s as well as a nod to the Spanish immigrants, once a vibrant part of the neighborhood.

Need some retail therapy? Head down to Bleecker Street where you will find some of New York's most charming brick and mortar shops. While shopping make sure to indulge your sweet tooth at the charmingly popular Magnolia Bakery, at 401 Bleecker. Head across the street to the Bleecker Playground to sit for a spell and indulge in that cupcake or long-line worthy banana pudding.

Bar Pisellino

"The Village" Checklist: See and Do

☐ Brunch at Dante West Village, 551 Hudson St.

☐ People watch in Washington Square Park.

☐ Cappuccino at Cafe Reggio, 119 MacDougal St.

☐ Buy flowers at Rosecrans, 7 Greenwich Ave.

☐ Magnolia Bakery for cupcakes, 401 Bleecker St.

☐ Browse for books at Three Lives & Co. Bookstore, 154 West 10th St.

☐ Drinks at Bar Pisellino, 52 Grove St.

☐ Take a peek into Grove Court, between 10 and 12 Grove St.

☐ Grab a slice of pizza at Joe's, 7 Carmine St.

☐ Snap a photo of Carrie Bradshaw's house, 64 Perry St.

☐ And the *Friends* apartment, 90 Bedford St.

East Village/
Lower East Side

East Village

The East Village has had an ever-shifting cast of residents: European immigrants in the early 1900s, a haven for artists, musicians, and writers starting in the 1950s, the epicenter of the city's punk scene in the 1970s, and more recently home to young professionals, families, and NYU students. But have no doubt, the neighborhood still maintains its colorful artistic spirit and eccentricity, setting it apart from other neighborhoods. It's filled with old-school spots, hip new restaurants, cafes, bars, unique shops, and some of the best vintage clothing stores in the city.

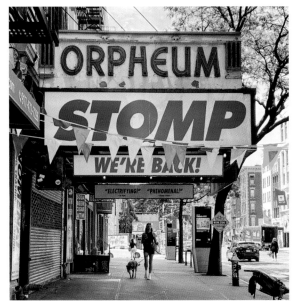

Get a Feel for the Neighborhood Old and New

To get a feeling of what the neighborhood was like back in the day, step into McSorley's Old Ale House, 15 East 7th St. Established in 1854 and the oldest Irish saloon in New York City, it has been a gathering place, a watering hole, and the subject of art, literature, and even a Supreme Court controversy. Everyone from Abe Lincoln to John Lennon has passed through its doors.

St. Mark's Church-in-the-Bowery, 131 East 10th St., not only is the oldest church of continuous worship in New York but has always been a progressive force in the neighborhood both socially and culturally. Supportive of immigrants, civil rights (the church was a meeting place for Black Panthers), and the arts, it's where Andy Warhol screened his early films.

Don't miss a stroll down what is arguably one of the most notable streets in the East Village, St. Mark's Place, between Third Avenue and Avenue A. The punk scene is long gone, but this street still maintains a gritty authentic feel.

If you are looking for a place to rest, refresh, and people watch, Tompkins Square Park on East 10th Street is the perfect spot. Once nearly bulldozed for being a dangerous, crime-ridden park, it is now the focal point of the neighborhood. The East Village and Lower East Side also contain the largest concentration of community gardens in the city, 39 out of a few hundred citywide.

Everywhere you look in the East Village you will find street art, the most famous being the Bowery Mural Wall at the corner of Houston and Bowery. Keith Haring painted his first iconic large-scale mural on this wall that has been a permanent fixture since 1982. It has evolved into a curated project with rotating artists both well known and emerging.

Hungry after walking the neighborhood? There are so many great spots to grab a bite, but I love Veselka, East 9th Street and Second Avenue, a 24-hour Ukrainian coffee shop famous for its authentic goulash, borscht, and pierogi. If you're looking for some lighter fare, across the street is MUD, a cute coffee shop with an all-day brunch and outdoor garden.

" A **BOOK** may well be the only TRUE *Magic*

— Alice Hoffman

the Strand Bookstore

Where else can you travel back in time, traverse the globe, step into imaginary worlds, or ponder the observations of the great historical and contemporary minds but in a fine-crafted book?

Favorite Independent Bookstores in NYC

THREE LIVES & COMPANY, 154 West 10th St.

THE STRAND, 12th Street and Broadway

ALBERTINE, 972 Fifth Ave.

MCNALLY JACKSON, 134 Prince St.

THE DRAMA BOOKSHOP, 266 West 39th St.

RIZZOLI BOOKSTORE, 26th Street and Broadway

192 BOOKS, 192 10th Ave.

THE MYSTERIOUS BOOKSHOP, 58 Warren St.

BONNIE SLOTNICK COOKBOOKS, 28 East 2nd St.

THE CORNER BOOKSTORE, 1313 Madison Ave.

Favorite East Village Shops

The East Village is home to so many amazing little independent shops. You'll delight in finding shops from a seemingly bygone era, where the salesperson is also the owner, designer, visual merchandiser, jack of all trades, and storyteller. A few of these include:

John Derian, 6 East 2nd St. Step into this store and you will feel as though you have left Manhattan and have been transported to a cozy shop on Paris's Left Bank. This home accessories shop is filled with Derian's decoupage glassware (paperweights, trays, dishes, etc.), vintage silverware, vibrant tablecloths, and beautiful furniture from around the world.

East Village Hats, 80 7th St. Walk into this tiny boutique and you're likely to see the owner and milliner Julia Emily Knox whipping up some gorgeous confection by hand or on her sewing machine in the back of the shop. Drawn by a stellar reputation spread by word of mouth, her customers come seeking unique, authentic pieces to elevate their wardrobe to the next level. They also offer workshops aimed at sharing the art of hat making.

Trash and Vaudeville, 96 East 7th St. Born out of the 1970s rock and punk scene on St. Mark's Place, Trash and Vaudeville has always provided a variety of alternative fashion for rockers, punks, goths, and everyday folk who just want to dress on the wild side.

9th St. Vintage, 346 East 9th St., specializes in pre-1960s clothing and Local Clothing, 328 E. 9th St., carries clothes from the 1980s and '90s.

La Sirena, 27 East 3rd St. This place makes my heart smile. Walking into La Sirena (which is Spanish for "mermaid") is like time traveling to a small village in Mexico with its explosion of color and floor-to-ceiling Mexican handicrafts, religious art, jewelry, puppets, charms, and more. Give yourself time to wander since you won't want to leave without a unique keepsake.

Le Bouquet, 116 East 4th St. One of the prettiest and most instagrammable flower shops in the city, this unique little spot features flowers for sale in the front and a Korean restaurant in the back.

Lower East Side

The Lower East Side (sometimes simply referred to as the "LES") is located between the Bowery and the East River from Canal to Houston Street. In the 19th and early 20th century, the LES was a beacon for newcomers to America with each group leaving its unique mark. Once known as "Little Germany" in the mid-1800s and home to more than a million Eastern European Jews in the early 1900s, today the area is a patchwork of different generations, cultures, longtime residents, and new transplants that make the neighborhood unique.

What was once row upon row of tenement buildings is now a mix of upscale apartments and chic boutiques. Though it's relatively quiet during the day, nighttime draws a hip, young crowd to the area's trendy bars, music venues, and restaurants. Orchard Street, which is often considered the center of the LES, closes to traffic on Sundays from Delancey to East Houston Streets. Crowds spill onto the streets, art galleries open their doors, and local shops set up tables and racks of their goods for passersby who might have some time to kill while waiting to snag a spot at Dudley's or Sunday to Sunday.

The best way to comprehend the heart of the LES history is by visiting one of the gems of the neighborhood, the Tenement Museum. Now a National Trust Historic Site at 103 Orchard St., this narrow, cramped building housed more than 7,000 immigrants between 1863 and 1935. For over two decades the restored museum has shown us what life was like during four different time periods in New York City.

Continue your sentimental journey with a taste of old New York at Katz's Deli, at 205 East Houston St. This New York institution has been serving up classic Jewish deli fare such as pastrami sandwiches and matzoh ball soup since 1888. (An insider's tip: Try to snag the infamous table from the film *When Harry Met Sally*. It's the best seat in the house.)

Just down the street is Russ & Daughters at 179 East Houston St. Line up with tourists and natives alike to order the best smoked fish, bagels, bialys, and babka.

Get your sugar fix at Economy Candy, 108 Rivington St., satisfying New Yorkers' sweet tooths since 1937. What started as a shoe repair shop with a candy cart in front quickly switched over to selling just candy. Today they sell over 2,000 varieties of sweets. If you can't find it here, it probably no longer exists.

SoHo / NoLita / Tribeca

SoHo

SoHo ("South of Houston") is bordered by Houston Street, Lafayette Street, and the western part of Broadway. In the mid-19th century SoHo was the heart of Manhattan's shopping, hotel, and entertainment district. Retail establishments such as Tiffany & Co. and Lord & Taylor got their start in this neighborhood. Theaters, music venues, and bars sprung up along Broadway. Long before SoHo became a bohemian artist enclave, brothels on Greene and Mercer Streets formed the city's first red-light district in the mid-1800s. The neighborhood was originally defined by manufacturing. Many of the beautiful cast iron buildings you see today were built for businesses that manufactured goods on the top floors and sold them in the ground floor shops.

By the 1950s the manufacturing trade moved to the suburbs and up-and-coming artists then moved into the neighborhood, favoring the open floor plans, high ceilings, and large windows of the abandoned industrial lofts. Galleries soon followed the artists and SoHo was once again transformed, this time into one of the most desirable and expensive areas of the city. As history always portends, space that was once the struggling artist's domain was over time turned into multi-million-dollar residential lofts. Many of the galleries are now high-end boutiques and trendy restaurants.

To see SoHo in its most vibrant spirit, you should plan to visit on a Saturday. The weekend is when the area really comes to life, when the fashion-conscious locals are joined by suburbanites and tourists looking to spend the day posing for pictures, dining alfresco, shopping, and gallery hopping. There's no particular strategy to touring SoHo—just pick a street and start wandering.

You will find something unique on every street in SoHo but a couple of my favorites include:

Crosby Street

The Crosby Street Hotel at 79 Crosby St. is situated in the heart of SoHo. At this whimsical boutique hotel, conversation pieces abound as art is a focal point in every space, from the floral arrangements to the whimsical dog sculptures (the hotel welcomes four-legged friends). Stop in for afternoon tea, finger sandwiches, and sweets on their outdoor terrace. Better yet, order a drink at the bar before heading off to one of the many neighborhood dining spots.

Housing Works Bookstore at 126 Crosby St. is a New York institution stocked with literary fiction, nonfiction, rare, and collectable books. Because all of their inventory is donated, and they are almost entirely staffed by volunteers, Housing Works donates 100 percent of their profits toward lifesaving services for people living with and affected by HIV/AIDS. Across the street is The Alchemist's Kitchen, which is part holistic cafe, part beauty and wellness boutique. They feature elixirs for inducing sweet dreams as well as for just about every ailment under the sun.

Greene Street

This 1-mile-long cobblestone/brick street is one of the most photogenic stretches of Soho. Replete with mid-19th-century architecture, here is where you will find not only high-end designer shops such as Fendi, Dior, and Versace but also one of the city's prettiest coffee shops, Felix Roasting Company at 104 Greene St., the perfect destination for artful espresso drinks, coffee cocktails, and sweet and savory pastries.

Prince Street

Prince Street is where you will find street vendors selling everything from jewelry-box worthy treasures to original artwork. Fanelli's Café at 94 Prince St. is the quintessential example of an old New York eatery. Beloved by artists and tourists alike, this 1847 watering hole is the second oldest food-and-drink establishment in the city. The best time to enjoy Fanelli's is in the morning hours before the crowds descend. Enjoy your breakfast sandwich along with the locals.

I always love a pretty green storefront, especially the kind where when you walk by you are completely intoxicated by the ever-seductive aroma of fresh baked bread wafting from its doorstep. Vesuvio Bakery at 160 Prince St. is just that and more. It sells the most delicious breads, sweets, and savories.

Just off Prince Street and on Thompson Street are two favorite shops of mine. The first is Julia Testa Flowers, 111 Thompson. Whether you're a flower lover, looking to send someone a gorgeous bouquet, or just want to see a pretty storefront, check it out. Across the street is a bespoke boutique for all hat lovers. The Hat Shop (120 Thompson) has something perfect for you whether you're a first-time buyer or self-confessed "hat addict." They also do custom design if for some reason you don't find what you're looking for.

Of course, there are other notable spots to eat in the neighborhood including Balthazar, at 80 Spring St. They serve everything from breakfast to special occasion dinners. The bakery features especially delightful, sweet treats, so be sure to make room for some indulgent nibbles. Dominique Ansel, at 189 Spring St., is best known for creating the "Cronut," the croissant-donut pastry which people still wait in line for. They also serve delicious avocado toast, quiche, and paninis.

Centre Street

If the City of Lights is on your bucket list but time and budget constraints preclude a trip to Paris for now, take a walk down Centre Street between Broome and Grand Streets. There you will notice French flags waving from shop fronts and little hand-painted blue and green signs affixed to planters and buildings that say, "Little Paris." For a moment you might think you've left the island of Manhattan way behind and are wandering around the streets of the Left Bank. The "Little Paris" designation is on track to become an official tittle for this particular stretch of NoLita/SoHo thanks to the founders of the local French language school named Coucou. Their goal is to establish a specific area of the city where Francophiles can find authentic French goods and experience a sense of French culture.

Start your French fantasy at Maman, located at 239 Centre St. Order a pain au chocolate and coffee or try one of their famous chocolate chip cookies. When you leave Maman, look across the street at one of New York's most beautiful and historic buildings, the Old Police Headquarters whose architecture was inspired by Paris's famous Hotel de Ville (City Hall). Several blocks from "Little Paris" are two of my favorite restaurants. La Mercerie, located at 53 Howard St., is the perfect spot to enjoy cafe classics during the day and cocktails in the evening, and Le Coucou at 138 Lafayette St. is a favorite of the in-the-know New York diners.

NoLita

While NoLita's name identifies it as being "North of Little Italy," this picturesque neighborhood has formed a distinct identity all its own. It is where you can go to escape the crowds of SoHo and Little Italy. Although it only spans a couple of blocks, it's packed with old-world charm. Spend a couple of hours roaming up and down Elizabeth, Mulberry, and Mott Streets absorbing the unique character of this neighborhood filled with pop-up art galleries, small independently owned shops, sidewalk cafes, and trendy restaurants.

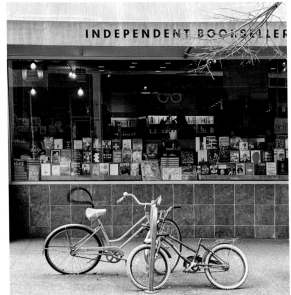

Elizabeth Street Garden

One of New York City's true gems, Elizabeth Street Garden is the perfect spot to find a bit of peace, quiet, and inspiration. Located between Prince and Spring Streets, this 1-acre sculpture garden is filled with ornate bird baths, lions carved from limestone, statues of Greek goddesses, and gargoyles strategically placed among stone benches, tables, perennial gardens, and two beautiful pear trees. While it's open to the public for now, sadly like most underdeveloped land in the city it is an endangered species, caught up in a political debate about whether the space should be used for more housing.

Other Favorite Spots in NoLita

Take a left out of the gardens and continue walking down Elizabeth Street where you will find remnants of the old neighborhood architecture and businesses blended with the new. Elizabeth Street Gallery and House of Hackney is a renovated 1850s NYC firehouse that is now an art gallery and British interior design firm. Albanese Meats and Poultry has been family owned and operated since 1923. It is one of only a handful of old-school butcher shops left in the city. Le Labo sells candles, lotions, and perfume that they hand blend while you wait. Love Adorned is the perfect place to pick up gifts. They carry an eclectic mix of new and vintage jewelry, dried flowers, and home goods. The shop is next to Tacombie Mexican restaurant, so you have a perfect excuse to take a margarita break.

Around the corner, at the intersection of Prince, Mott, and Mulberry Streets, is a bit of New York history. Constructed in the mid-1800s, St. Patrick's Old Cathedral was the former cathedral of the Archdiocese of New York as well as an important community center for newly arrived immigrants. Head down Mulberry to The Meadow, a tiny shop that specializes in gourmet salt, artisanal chocolate from around the world, bitters, and fresh cut flowers. Pop in next door to Goods for the Study, dedicated to all things involved in creating the perfect workspace: pens, stationery, notebooks, etc. For all you book lovers, McNally Jackson, one of New York's favorite literary hubs, is down the street at 134 Prince St.

For such a small neighborhood, there is no shortage of places to dine. Café Gitano at 242 Mott St. and Epistrophy at 200 Mott St. are two great brunch and people-watching spots.

Tribeca

With its understated elegance and gritty industrial vibe from an era long gone, this neighborhood is the epitome of downtown cool. The "Triangle Below Canal" area is known for its unique mashup of architecture, blending towering high-rise buildings with meticulously restored factory and loft spaces. Spectacular views of the Hudson River on its western border along with notable restaurants, shopping, luxury hotels, and the Tribeca Film Festival have made this area a certified celebrity hotspot.

Tribeca: See and Do

Walk by 14 North Moore St. any time of day and you are sure to see people standing outside of FDNY Ladder 8 taking photos. If you're a pop-culture lover or fan of the classic *Ghostbusters* movie, this is the same firehouse featured as the group's headquarters. Built in 1903, this Beaux-Arts beauty is a working firehouse so there's no going inside. However, if the door just happens to be open, you can pop your head inside to catch a glimpse of the original *Ghostbusters* sign.

Staple Street, located at 9 Jay St., may seem like any other alleyway in the city, but this street is one of the smallest streets in Manhattan, measuring just 2 blocks. It features a unique remnant from a bygone era—look up and you will see one of the few remaining cast iron skybridges suspended between two buildings. This bridge was built as a pedestrian walkway in 1907 to connect New York Hospital's emergency room with their laundry facility. More recently a high-profile fashion designer used the skybridge to connect his apartment to his design studio. Now that's what I call a seamless commute.

Where else but in New York can you find a book shop that has floor-to-ceiling stacks of books specializing in fictitious tales of crime, espionage, whodunits, and the biggest collection of Sherlock Holmes books in the world? The Mysterious Bookshop (such an appropriate name!) is at 58 Warren St. Another unique shop just a couple of doors down is the Philip Williams Poster Museum. It's part gallery and part retail shop with over 100,000 unique posters dating from the 1870s to the present all carefully curated by category. Poster art may not always be recognized for its "importance," but posters are truly an intrinsic part of our lives and history. They hung in our bedrooms when we were kids, and we pass by them daily on walls of subways and buildings.

End your day at Aire Ancient Baths in the heart of Tribeca at 88 Franklin St. This spa is dedicated to the relaxation of body and mind, inspired by the legacy of Greek and Roman baths. The gorgeous space promotes a sense of calm. There are serene thermal waters in contrasting temperatures and for an extra treat, splurge on a massage or special olive oil ritual. Pure, peaceful bliss!

Lower Manhattan

Lower Manhattan

Lower Manhattan—with the heart of the nation's financial markets, cultural landmarks, soaring skyscrapers, and an instantly recognizable skyline—is also the oldest neighborhood in New York City. The neighborhood is a study in contrast, from the stunning modern architecture of The Oculus NYC transportation hub to the curvy cobblestone alleyway of Stone Street.

In recent years Lower Manhattan has seen its share of tragedy and triumph. From the heartbreaking devastation of the 9/11 terrorist attacks to the wreckage left behind by Hurricane Sandy, the area and its people have always bounced back with tremendous resolve and perseverance.

There is something here to see and do for everybody, from the history buff to the hardcore shopper and everything in between.

When exploring Lower Manhattan, I like to start at The Battery (also known as Battery Park). Here you will find sweeping panoramic views of the New York Harbor and Lady Liberty, a beautiful carousel, outdoor cafes, perennial gardens, and several interesting small museums and memorials. This is also the docking area where you can pick up the ferry to visit the Statue of Liberty and Ellis Island. Be sure to check out one of the lesser-known memorials in the park, the Irish Hunger Memorial, on the corner of Vesey and North End Avenue.

Take a walk down Wall Street, which isn't merely a street. As New York's financial district, it is also synonymous with the world of money and business. Trinity Church stands at the head of Wall Street; its Gothic spire served as a guide for ships entering the New York Harbor. It is also the burial site of Alexander Hamilton. Lower Manhattan has plenty of outdoor art to behold including a couple of high-profile sculptures, *Fearless Girl* and *Charging Bull*. Word has it that rubbing the bull brings good luck.

Experience the culinary side of old-world New York at historic spots such as Fraunces Tavern, Delmonico's, and Stone Street, with its quaint cobblestone foundation full of pubs and restaurants.

The Oculus NYC is a memorial, transportation hub, and shopping center all in one. Designed by world-renowned architect Santiago Calatrava, the space is intended to resemble a bird flying from the hand of a child, a symbol of hope and new beginnings after the 9/11 attacks.

Across from the Oculus is the 9/11 Memorial and Museum. Every American should visit this memorial at least once. As you enter the museum you descend from street level to the foundation of the former Twin Towers. Through oral recordings, still images, moving images, and more than 14,000 objects, it pays homage to the enormity of loss both physical and spiritual. It is at once gut-wrenching and beautiful.

The South Street Seaport and Pier 17 are home to the Seaport Museum and the city's largest concentration of restored maritime buildings. It was the first 24-hour district in New York, hence the phrase "the city that never sleeps." In the last couple of years, it has become a hotspot of great restaurants, bars, art, architecture, shopping, and entertainment.

Take a stroll over one of NYC's most historic and recognizable bridges, the Brooklyn Bridge. Stretching a little over a mile, it was the longest suspension bridge when it was completed in 1883. It became a symbol of optimism and possibility. Enjoy the scenic views while also envisioning a drool-worthy slice of Brooklyn's famous Grimaldi's pizza that awaits you on the other side.

Make sure you don't pass up one of New York's best bargains—a ride on the Staten Island Ferry. The ferry departs every 15 to 30 minutes from the Whitehall terminal on South Street. The 25-minute ride takes you past the Statue of Liberty with views of the boroughs of Manhattan and Staten Island along with astonishing skylines in either direction. The best part is, it's FREE!!!!

Fun Fact

When the Brooklyn Bridge was built in 1883, New Yorkers were fearful and skeptical that the bridge couldn't sustain the weight of the commuters expected to use it. In an effort to ease the public's concern, the city asked circus showman P .T. Barnum to demonstrate the strength of the bridge by parading 21 elephants across its expanse. The rest, as they say, is history!

BUCKET LIST for LOWER MANHATTAN

New York
The City that Never Sleeps

Ferry over to the Statue of Liberty
Rub the Charging Bull for Good Luck
Walk down Wall Street
Visit the 9/11 Memorial and Museum
Admire the Oculus Architecture
Dine on Stone Street
Take a Free Ride on the Staten Island Ferry
Walk the Brooklyn Bridge
Step back in time at South Street Seaport

GEMS OF NEW YORK

New York Flower District

The New York Flower District

When it comes to buying flowers, I ascribe to the school of thought that says that no matter the occasion—or better, yet no occasion at all—a perfect posy is one of life's greatest pleasures. Whether you're the sender or the receiver, nothing conveys romance, support, congratulations, or simply "I'm thinking of you" quite like a floral bouquet.

One of the best places to find beautiful fresh flowers for much less than the price of your local florist is the New York Flower District, on West 28th Street between Sixth and Seventh Avenue. There you will amble through a labyrinth of wholesale shops where potted plants, trees, and flowers in every color of the rainbow vie for the attention of the discerning eyes of designers, decorators, event planners, and you.

The New York Flower District dates to the late 19th century, when immigrants from Eastern Europe identified an untapped market and began providing flowers for department stores, funerals, and steamships. At one time, the market had more than 60 vendors, and by the late 1970s, New York was second only to Amsterdam in the number of flowers bought and sold daily. Alas, although the changing times and skyrocketing rents have dramatically reduced the size of the market over the years, it nevertheless retains its delightful, enchanting spirit.

Fun Fact

The Daffodil Project is a citywide planting by residents and volunteers of hundreds of thousands of daffodil bulbs donated annually as a living memorial to those lost on September 11th. In 2007 Mayor Michael Bloomberg announced that the daffodil, one of the most beautiful and dependable harbingers of spring, was the official flower of New York City.

Guidelines for Navigating the District

The Flower District operates Monday through Saturday with most shops opening around 5 a.m. The earliest vendors sell exclusively to wholesale customers. As the morning unfolds, the market opens to the general public. I like to get there around 7:30 a.m., just in time to observe the peak of activity. Being in the midst of all the hustle and bustle is the best part about exploring the district. The Flower District usually shuts down for the day around lunchtime.

Bring cash as not all shops accept credit cards.

Dress comfortably. You'll be leaning over sidewalk flower displays, maneuvering through narrow shop aisles, stepping over leaves and stray petals on the pavement, and dodging nursery trucks pulling up from every direction with sellers hauling trees and potted plants across the street with no regard to pedestrians.

There are many shops on each side of the street, and each with its own unique personality, one seemingly more stunning than the next. Take a mental inventory of what's available at the various stores, then loop back to each shop to collect your picks.

If you are buying multiple bunches and want to browse more comfortably, you can stash your flowers on shelves located in the back of most shops.

Bring your camera. You'll want to take photos to keep track of what you see as you go from shop to shop in case you want to go back and buy. Moreover, you'll have a colorful keepsake photo of the Flower District when you need a memorable pick-me-up on a dreary day.

Best time of year to go? Anytime as there is always something magical every season of the year at the Flower District.

Art in Transit

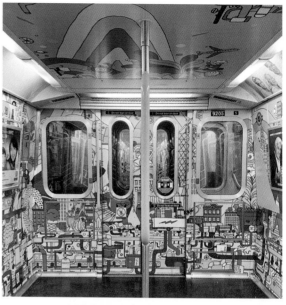

Art in Transit

Have you ever noticed as you navigate your way through New York's subways that the beautiful artwork in the city isn't always above ground? Take a moment before you make a mad dash for the subway and experience a first-rate art museum at most any stop, comprised of works created in mosaic, terra-cotta, bronze, glass, mixed media, and sculpture. The artwork was all created by the MTA Arts & Design program established in 1985 when the subway system was making a concerted effort to reverse years of decline. Arts & Design commissions public art that is seen by the hundreds of thousands of city-dwellers, commuters, and national and international visitors who travel by the New York City Transit system every day. As the MTA rehabilitates subway stations, it uses a portion of its funds to commission permanent works of art. Arts & Design projects create links to neighborhoods with art that echoes the architectural history and design of the individual locations.

Some of My Favorite Subway Station Artwork

Perfect Strangers, by artist Vik Muniz, 72nd Street and Second Avenue. *Perfect Strangers* is a series of three dozen life-size portraits that seem to be waiting for a train along the concourse and entrances of the station. The artwork is based on staged photographs of people the artist knows.

Stationary Figures, by artist William Wegman at the 23rd Street (F line) station features the artist's Weimaraners Flo and Topper. Immortalized in 11 glass mosaic panels, the dogs take on human attributes from wearing street clothes to being grouped like passengers as they peer down the platform as if waiting for the train.

Carrying On, by artist Janet Zweig, at Prince Street (R train) station is composed of almost two hundred silhouettes of people hauling "stuff" with them as they walk the streets of New York. Begun after the 9/11 tragedy, it represents New Yorkers literally "carrying on" with their lives. The artist worked from photos of individuals moving about, in and out of the subway, always carrying something, from the sublime to the ridiculous. The result is a linear narrative work of miniature figures, each of whom has a story to tell.

Broadway Diary, by artist Timothy Snell at the 8th Street-NYU station (R train). Artist Tim Snell says, "the mosaic is composed of 40 portholes that depict scenes and historic sites of the neighborhood (Grace Church, Washington Square Arch, Cooper Union, Astor Place)." The artwork is spread out in an architectural format throughout the station integrating the artwork with the space.

Roaming Underfoot, by artist Nancy Blum at the 28th Street (IRT East Side line). Glass mosaic murals grace the platform walls of the historic 28th Street station. The artwork depicts seven flowering blooms inspired by nearby Madison Square Park's Perennial Collection. The flowers include daffodils, magnolias, hydrangea, and witch hazel, chosen as a representation of plant species that withstand the changing climate conditions of the city.

Memories of Twenty-Third Street, by artist Keith Goddard at 23rd Street (R train) station. From the 1800s through the 1920s, 23rd Street was a major vaudeville, entertainment, and cultural district. "Ladies' Mile," the fashion and department store haven of the time, was located nearby. In his mosaics, Keith Goddard represents the area through various hats that pedestrians sported back in the day. Both everyday citizens and celebrities of the time (Oscar Wilde, Eleanor Roosevelt, Thomas Edison, Sarah Bernhardt, Houdini) are highlighted.

The Revelers, by artist Jane Dickson at Times Square and 42nd Street station. Times Square is known for many things, most notably its crowds, especially during the spirited celebration on New Year's Eve. *The Revelers*, 70 expressive, life-size figures each depicted in some form of motion (walking, dancing, linking arms) are seen celebrating New Year's Eve in Times Square.

The Holidays

New York City's Greatest Production of All

There is nothing New Yorkers love more than a celebration.

It all begins on New Year's Eve when an estimated one million people descend upon Times Square to watch the ball drop and ring in the New Year. On March 17th, every New Yorker feels just a "wee bit Irish" once the traditional green line is painted down the middle of Fifth Avenue, the location of the world's oldest and largest St. Patrick's Day parade. A few weeks later, also on Fifth Avenue, is the Easter Parade—a literal 8-block runway of dandies and swells strutting their Easter bonnet best ranging from the sublime to the outrageous. The month of June is filled with Pride festivities throughout the city, and then there's the annual Macy's 4th of July fireworks display bursting upon the city's two rivers amidst the wide-eyed "oohs" and "aahs" of the appreciative crowds lining the shore.

As summer reluctantly gives way to fall, there is something magical that begins to happen in late September. There is an intangible, imperceptible shift in the air—but make no mistake, it's there. Autumn in New York arrives unabashedly in all her splendiferous collection of breathtaking beauty. The Union Square Market has the feel of a North Fork, Long Island pumpkin patch with its profusion of apples; bittersweet, fresh-made donuts; sunflowers; bales of hay; cornstalks; mums; and naturally pumpkins of all sizes, shapes, and colors. Seemingly overnight from the East Side to the West Side, scary, cozy, and uber-creative Halloween décor takes over the city. Goblins, ghosts, and massive spiders appear in hidden doorways, townhouse stoops, apartment building lobbies, restaurants, and parks. There are endless activities to partake in during this spectacularly spooky season: pumpkin painting in the South Street Seaport, ghost walks in the West Village, candlelight tours at the Merchant House Museum. The festivities culminate on Halloween night at the annual Village Halloween Parade where more than 50,000 zombies, ghouls, witches, monsters, and giant puppets take to the streets for a night of revelry.

The curtain is about to rise—let the holidays begin!

Santa's Arrival

The culmination of the annual Thanksgiving Day Parade is also the most anticipated for millions of boys and girls (and adults). Santa's arrival into Herald Square officially marks the most joyful, magical, and fun-filled time of year. The holiday season is here at last!

Christmastime in the city is like no other. It's in the air, it's in the hustle and bustle on the streets, the jewel-like sparkling of Christmas trees peeking out of apartment windows, the numerous outdoor holiday markets dotting the city landscape, as well as the myriad decorations in office lobbies and shops. Familiar, memory-filled smells and sounds pervade the senses: pine mixed with gingerbread and peppermint, hot chocolate, roasting chestnuts, church bells, Christmas tunes echoing in the chilly night air, and excited laughter of gleeful children.

City sidewalks are busy sidewalks as locals and tourists alike navigate their way down Fifth Avenue strolling by decorative store windows, having their photo taken in front of the famous Rockefeller Center tree, waiting in line at FAO Schwarz toy store, or heading to the Christmas Spectacular at Radio City Music Hall.

Restaurants, cafes, and bars go all out on holiday décor, from the elegant Tavern on the Green to the over-the-top explosion of holiday spirit at Rolf's German Restaurant. With 100,000 lights, 15,000 ornaments, and thousands of icicles hanging from the rafters of this cozy eatery—well, if this place doesn't get you into the holiday spirit then nothing will! When you're there, make sure you try the spiced eggnog or a glass of their famous mulled wine. After a day of window shopping, sightseeing, and just breathing in the city in all its festive finery, you'll be glad you did.

New York during the holiday season—truly "The Most Wonderful Time of the Year"!

The Christmas Tree Vendors

What would New York be during the holiday season without the delightfully visual scene and intoxicatingly fresh scent of newly cut fir trees propped up against sheds decked in twinkling lights, wreaths, and homemade decorations?

While most of us are finishing up the last of the Thanksgiving pumpkin pie, the Christmas tree sellers are making their way down from Canada, Vermont, and Upstate New York by the truckloads. In only a matter of days, festive-minded New Yorkers will carry their newly purchased trees through the streets and into their homes to kick off the holidays. I've seen every size tree tied to the top of yellow cabs, rigged up to the back of a Citi bike, and a few even held precariously in the back of a pedicab. New Yorkers are endlessly creative in all pursuits!

The Christmas tree vendors have been a longstanding tradition in the city. For one month every year they become part of the neighborhood, creating a small-town ambiance in an otherwise urban jungle. Some of the tree sellers return to the same neighborhood year after year forming a bond with the local residents and small businesses who supply them with warm coffee, home-cooked meals, a place to do laundry, and simply, someone to chat with on a cold winter's day. Tens of thousands of trees are sold throughout the city from the day after Thanksgiving until December 24th, and as quickly as they arrive, they disappear until the next year. The last vestiges of pine needles on the sidewalk never fail to pull at my heartstrings.

Cheers to the Christmas tree vendors who fill the city sidewalks with holiday spirit, joy, and Christmas cheer!

Rocky: The Christmas Miracle of 2020

As Christmas 2020 was approaching, the world was cast in the shadows of a devastating tragedy. The Big Apple—one of the quintessential destinations as a "Christmas city"—was now the epicenter of the raging virus. Where the streets would normally be filled with merry-making tourists, city sidewalks would be "busy sidewalks, dressed in holiday style," in truth and in the air there was little "feelings of Christmas." Even Santa Claus's annual headquarters at Macy's Department Store, visited by children from around the world for decades, was forced to shut down.

And yet, in the midst of so much sadness there was a silver lining (or, should we call it "feathered" lining) . . . a story that could have been written by the master of Christmas tales, Charles Dickens. However, this was not a fairy tale, but was in fact, a real-life little saga about a winged being who was destined to bring some much-needed hope and magic to our city.

While so many of our treasured traditions were canceled during this time, the annual arrival of the Rockefeller Center Christmas tree, a New York institution since the Great Depression, carried on. As the massive 75-foot Norway spruce was being hoisted onto its iconic place of grandeur, one of the workers who had helped transport and was now lighting the tree spotted a tiny saw-whet owl (one of the smallest in the world) tucked inside its branches. Having traveled a 3-day, 170-mile journey from its original Upstate New York home with no food or water, this sweet, tiny owl was now unknowingly immersed in the bright lights, strange smells, and loud noises of the big city. Little could this frightened owl know what an impact she would have on the people of New York. Word quickly spread and she would eventually be named "Rocky" (short for "Rockefeller"). Rocky became a symbol of hope and resilience in a time when we needed it most; she was our Christmas Miracle. Eventually Rocky was taken to a wildlife center, treated with lots of TLC, and released to head back home to a long and happy life.

December "Musts" in NYC

- [ ] Visit the tree at Rockefeller Center
- [ ] See the Radio City Christmas Spectacular
- [ ] Shop for gifts at Bryant Park Holiday Market
- [ ] Meet friends at Lillie's Victorian for holiday drinks
- [ ] Visit Santa at Macy's (no matter how old you are)
- [ ] Go skating in Central Park
- [ ] Book afternoon tea at the Plaza Hotel
- [ ] Admire the Fifth Avenue holiday window displays
- [ ] Take a carriage ride through Central Park
- [ ] Have a festive dinner at Rolf's

☐ Order a holiday cake from Magnolia Bakery

☐ Get tickets to New York City Ballet's *Nutcracker*

☐ Admire the city's holiday lights from above at Top of the Rock

☐ Pick up Christmas ornaments at John Derian

☐ Take the family to see the Big Apple Circus at Lincoln Center

☐ Shop the Flower Market for Christmas poinsettias

☐ Bask in the glow of the tree at the Met Museum

☐ Slurp frozen hot chocolate at Serendipity 3

☐ Stop into Greenwich Letterpress for holiday cards

☐ Attend a reading of *A Christmas Carol* at the Merchant House Museum

☐ Head to Washington Square Park for caroling on Christmas Eve

Acknowledgments

This book is dedicated to my favorite New Yorker of all, my husband.
THANK YOU for always being my biggest cheerleader. You are the apple of my eye.

This book is my homage to my hometown, the city that never sleeps.
New York, you are magical, messy, quizzical, and quirky, yet perfect in every way!

A heartfelt thank you to my parents Bette and Ed
for never missing an opportunity to introduce all nine of their kids to the wonders of the
"Big Apple," from Uptown to Downtown and everywhere in-between.

Thank you to my sister Maryclaire Sullivan
for her expert edits, beautiful way with words, encouragement, and love.

Thank you to artist Arielle Pearl,
who enthusiastically helped make my dream of getting this book off the ground a reality
with her beautiful proposal design. I couldn't have done it without you.

I was so lucky to work with three amazing New York City artists:
Tracey Berglund, Arielle Pearl, and Katie Woodward.
Thank you for your unique and flawless interpretations of NYC.

Thank you, Amy Lyons at Globe Pequot, for thinking my submission was a good idea for a book
and Greta Schmitz for jumping in and seeing it through.

About the Author

DEIRDRE GARTNER was born and raised in the city of New York. She brings a uniquely personal and distinct perspective to the city that she adores.

As a former fashion executive traveling the globe for years, nothing was more affirming and inspiring than when she would return home to Manhattan. Informed by her adventures abroad, this native daughter's ardor and curiosity for all things New York led her to zealously document both the obvious and hidden that the city has to offer.

Gartner's extensive collection of lovingly curated photographs, stories, and historical details eventually led to the creation of the "Girl in the Yellow Taxi NYC" website and Instagram. Her work has been featured in Condé Nast India, the New York Board of Tourism, StreetEasy, and others. She has been a guest blogger for various websites and has created custom itineraries for her enthusiastic international and domestic followers.

About the Artists

TRACEY BERGLUND is an illustrator based in Hell's Kitchen. Her work has been published in the *New Yorker*, *McSweeney's*, and the *New York Times*. She travels the world for clients such as the United Nations, IBM, and Google, but no matter where she is in the world Tracey believes that for her there is no place better to be than NYC.

ARIELLE PEARL is an artist and lifelong New Yorker who works as a designer and animator at Penguin Random House. Combining her love of storytelling and design, her illustrations have been featured on book titles such as *A Clash of Kings: The Graphic Novel: Volumes One–Four* by George R. R. Martin and *My Name is Venus Black* by Heather Lloyd. She loves collaborating with small businesses and lending her services to individuals on independent design projects. In her free time you can find Arielle with her husband and dogs, spending time in nature, and traveling with family and friends.

KATIE WOODWARD is a watercolor artist and proud Brooklyn resident. Art has been a lifelong pastime for Katie, and her professional background includes painting scenery and props for theater. She is the author of *The Urban Sketching Handbook: Understanding Light*. Katie can often be found urban sketching around New York, playing shuffleboard, hanging with friends in Prospect Park, and attempting to keep her growing collection of houseplants alive.